MEET THE SPINOSAURUS

Fun Facts & Cool Pictures

Julian Hawking

Table of Contents

Meet the Spinosaurus: The Most Mysterious Dinosaur to Walk the Earth

Can you imagine an animal the size of a dinosaur with a long, crocodile-like head and a massive fan-shaped hump of many colors? Think of it as one animal with features of a camel, crocodile, and a dinosaur. What you are imagining is a special dinosaur known as the Spinosaurus. The name Spinosaurus means "spine lizard," and that name fits perfectly, since this dinosaur shared many features with crocodiles that are alive today.

The Spinosaurus is believed to have thrived on land and in water in North Africa, Egypt, and Morocco. What makes this dinosaur special is the fact that scientists know very little about its life. Most of the fossil remains believed to be in existence have not yet been found. That means everything we think we know about this mysterious animal may one day be proven untrue.

Even though we don't know everything about the Spinosaurus, there are some things you can learn about this colorful dinosaur. Keep reading to learn what a Spinosaurus may have eaten for dinner and other interesting information.

When the Spinosaurus Walked the Earth

The Spinosaurus lived approximately 100 million years ago during a period of time known as the Cretaceous Period. During this period of time, the earth had more large bodies of water than it has today, so there were many large animals living in the water and on land, including the Spinosaurus.

Flowering plants first started to populate the earth during this period of time.

The Cretaceous Period came right after the Jurassic Period, which was known for its large dinosaur population. It is believed that the Cretaceous Period was the last period of life for dinosaurs, so the Spinosaurus lived right before dinosaur extinction occurred.

Scientists believe that Spinosaurus lived in the middle of the Cretaceous Period. This is how it is estimated that it lived approximately 100 million years ago.

Picture the Spinosaurus

If a Spinosaurus came walking down your street right now, the first thing you would notice would be the colorful fan-shaped hump sticking up from its back. This hump was made from long spines connected together by fat or skin. The spines are believed to have been five feet in length, if not longer.

This hump is often referred to as a “sail.” Scientists believe that the sail was brightly colored. The colors may have helped the dinosaur attract mates, but the sail was more likely used for self-defense. You will learn more about that when you read about the Spinosaurus in Action.

The Spinosaurus was one of the biggest dinosaurs ever to walk the earth. It was probably 40–60 feet long and may have weighed as much as 23 tons. It had four legs, but it probably walked upright on its back two legs much of the time.

One unusual physical feature of the Spinosaurus was its head, which looked much like the head of crocodiles we see on earth today. Maybe it seems silly that a dinosaur would have a crocodile's head, but it makes sense when you remember that the earth had a lot of water during this time period and that the Spinosaurus spent a lot of time in swamps.

Spinosaurus in Action

Scientists believe that the Spinosaurus was able to extend its sail to full length whenever it wanted. This would make the animal look much larger than it truly was, which may have made it more threatening to other animals. This would have been a powerful skill when fighting off enemies—although it is believed that the Spinosaurus did not have many enemies due to its size. The colorful sail may also have been used to attract mates.

Spinosaurus skeletons have shown that these animals had joints similar to human joints. Joints are what allow your arms and legs to bend and move. If this dinosaur had joints in its back, it would have been able to bend and arch its back much like we humans move our bodies today.

If the Spinosaurus ever got into a foot race with other dinosaurs, there is a good chance it would have won. Scientists believe it could go as fast as 15 miles per hour, and that was very fast considering how big this dinosaur was.

Spinosaurus Senses: What Were Its Strengths?

Since the Spinosaurus had a long spout like a crocodile, it probably hunted much like a crocodile. It may have had a strong sense of smell, which it could have used to sniff out dead animals to scavenge for food. It may have also had great eyesight, which it would have used to spot and grab fish in the water.

What's for Dinner?

(Photo by Spencer Wright)

The Spinosaurus used it size to hunt smaller dinosaurs and other animals that lived during the Cretaceous Period. Scientists believe they may have also dined on fish. Since this dinosaur ate meat, we would call it a carnivore.

Would a Spinosaurus Want to Be Your Friend?

Since few remains of the Spinosaurus have been found, scientists are not sure about their social habits. Fossil remains often leave clues as to whether dinosaurs traveled in groups or alone as well as how they cared for younger animals. The fossils that have been found for this dinosaur do not provide this information, so you may never know whether the Spinosaurus would have been your friend or your enemy.

Spinosaurus Lifespan

Scientists do not know with certainty how long the Spinosaurus might have lived. Many estimate they could have lived 50–100 years based on their size, but there is no clear evidence to prove this lifespan.

What the Spinosaurus Left Behind

(Photo by Kabacchi)

Spinosaurus fossils have been discovered in North Africa, Egypt, and Morocco, but the complete remains of a whole

Spinosaurus have yet to be found. Scientists believe that the Sahara Desert in Africa contains many Spinosaurus fossils, but it is difficult to dig them up because the desert is so hot and dry.

(Photo by Kabacchi)

The very first Spinosaurus fossils found were dug out of the earth in 1912. Those remains were destroyed in a battle during World War II, but the notes describing the remains were not destroyed. Much of what we now believe about this dinosaur comes from scientists studying those notes rather than the actual dinosaur remains.

(Photo by Kabacchi)

More recent discoveries include the vertebrae of a Spinosaurus dug up in 2011. These vertebrae revealed the long spout similar to the crocodiles we know today. This is how we know that this dinosaur likely shared head features with the crocodile.

Weird Spinosaurus Facts

- It is believed that Spinosaurus used their large sails to control their body temperature. Without the sail, they may not have been able to keep their bodies cool in the hot African deserts. And when temperatures dropped, they may not have been able to keep their bodies warm without the sail.

- Paleontologists are scientists who study fossil remains of animals. The Spinosaurus is of great interest to paleontologists who study dinosaur remains because so few remains have been found. Since scientists cannot directly study the fossil remains of the animal, much of what they believe about this dinosaur is uncertain. That makes the Spinosaurus one of the most mysterious animals to ever walk the earth.

Spinosaurus in Our World Today

The Spinosaurus has appeared in some animated documentaries exploring the lives of the most menacing dinosaurs to walk the earth, including features televised by BBC and Animal Planet. The Spinosaurus' part in the movie Jurassic Park 3 was the biggest appearance for this dinosaur in our modern world.

Due to its size and power, the Spinosaurus is also included in many dinosaur war games. Different dinosaurs are analyzed for their unique features, and then gamers try to determine who would win in a battle between different combinations of dinosaurs. These wars were started by the Jurassic Park movies, which featured many dinosaur battles, including one between a Spinosaurus and T-rex.

Other Books In This Series

Did you know that there are other dinosaur books in this series that you might enjoy?

Meet The T-Rex

Meet The Velociraptor

Meet The Pterodactyl

Meet The Stegosaurus

Meet The Triceratops

Meet The Brachiosaurus

Made in United States
Orlando, FL
15 November 2021